MW01041509

BASKETBALL LEGENDS

Kareem Abdul-Jabbar

Charles Barkley

Larry Bird

Wilt Chamberlain

Clyde Drexler

Julius Erving

Patrick Ewing

Anfernee Hardaway

The Head Coaches

Grant Hill

Juwan Howard

Allen Iverson

Magic Johnson

Michael Jordan

Shawn Kemp

Jason Kidd

Reggie Miller

Alonzo Mourning

Hakeem Olajuwon

Shaquille O'Neal

Gary Payton

Scottie Pippen

David Robinson

Dennis Rodman

John Stockton

CHELSEA HOUSE PUBLISHERS

BASKETBALL LEGENDS

ALONZO MOURNING

Bert Rosenthal

Introduction by
Chuck Daly

CHELSEA HOUSE PUBLISHERS
Philadelphia

Designed by Combined Publishing
Conshohocken, Pennsylvania

Cover illustration by Bradford Brown

First Printing

1 3 5 7 9 8 6 4 2

Library of Congress Cataloging-in-Publication Data

Rosenthal, Bert.
    Alonzo Mourning / by Bert Rosenthal.
            p. cm. — (Basketball legends)
    Includes bibliographic references (p.) and index.
    Summary: Presents the "rags-to-riches" story of Alonzo Mourning,
from his humble beginnings in an orphanage to college star in
Georgetown basketball to his $100 million contract with the Miami Heat.
    ISBN 0-7910-4577-3 (hardcover)
    1. Mourning, Alonzo, 1970- —Juvenile literature. 2. Basketball
players—United States—Biography—Juvenile literature.
[1. Mourning, Alonzo, 1970-   . 2. Basketball players. 3. Afro-
Americans—Biography.] I. Title. II. Series.
GV884.M65R67 1998
796.323'092—dc21
    [b]   97-46624
                                                            CIP
                                                             AC

CONTENTS

BECOMING A BASKETBALL LEGEND

Chuck Daly

What does it take to be a basketball superstar? Two of the three things it takes are easy to spot. Any great athlete must have excellent skills and tremendous dedication. The third quality needed is much harder to define, or even put in words. Others call it leadership or desire to win, but I'm not sure that explains it fully. This third quality relates to the athlete's thinking process, a certain mentality and work ethic. One can coach athletic skills, and while few superstars need outside influence to help keep them dedicated, it is possible for a coach to offer some well-timed words in order to keep that athlete fully motivated. But a coach can do no more than appeal to a player's will to win; how much that player is then capable of ensuring victory is up to his own internal workings.

In recent times, we have been fortunate to have seen some of the best to play the game. Larry Bird, Magic Johnson, and Michael Jordan had all three components of superstardom in full measure. They brought their teams to numerous championships, and made the players around them better. (They also made their coaches look smart.)

I myself coached a player who belongs in that class, Isiah Thomas, who helped lead the Detroit Pistons to consecutive NBA crowns. Isiah is not tall—he's just over six feet—but he could do whatever he wanted with the ball. And what he wanted to do most was lead and win.

All the players I mentioned above and those whom this series will chronicle are tremendously gifted athletes, but for the most part, you can't play professional basketball at all unless you have excellent skills. And few players get to stay on their team unless they are willing to dedicate themselves to improving their talents even more, learning about their opponents, and finding a way to join with their teammates and win.

It's that third element that separates the good player from the superstar, the memorable players from the legends of the game. Superstars know when to take over the game. If the situation calls for a defensive stop, the superstars stand up and do it. If the situation calls for a key pass, they make it. And if the situation calls for a big shot, they want the ball. They don't want the ball simply because of their own glory or ego. Instead they know—and their teammates know—that they are the ones who can deliver, regardless of the pressure.

The words "legend" and "superstar" are often tossed around without real meaning. Taking a hard look at some of those who truly can be classified as "legends" can provide insight into the things that brought them to that level. All of them developed their legacy over numerous seasons of play, even if certain games will always stand out in the memories of those who saw them. Those games typically featured amazing feats of all-around play. No matter how great the fans thought the superstars were, these players were capable of surprising the fans, their opponents, and occasionally even themselves. The desire to win took over, and with their dedication and athletic skills already in place, they were capable of the most astonishing achievements.

CHUCK DALY, now the head coach of the Orlando Magic, guided the Detroit Pistons to two straight NBA championships, in 1989 and 1990. He earned a gold medal as coach of the 1992 U.S. Olympic basketball team—the so-called "Dream Team"—and was inducted into the Pro Basketball Hall of Fame in 1994.

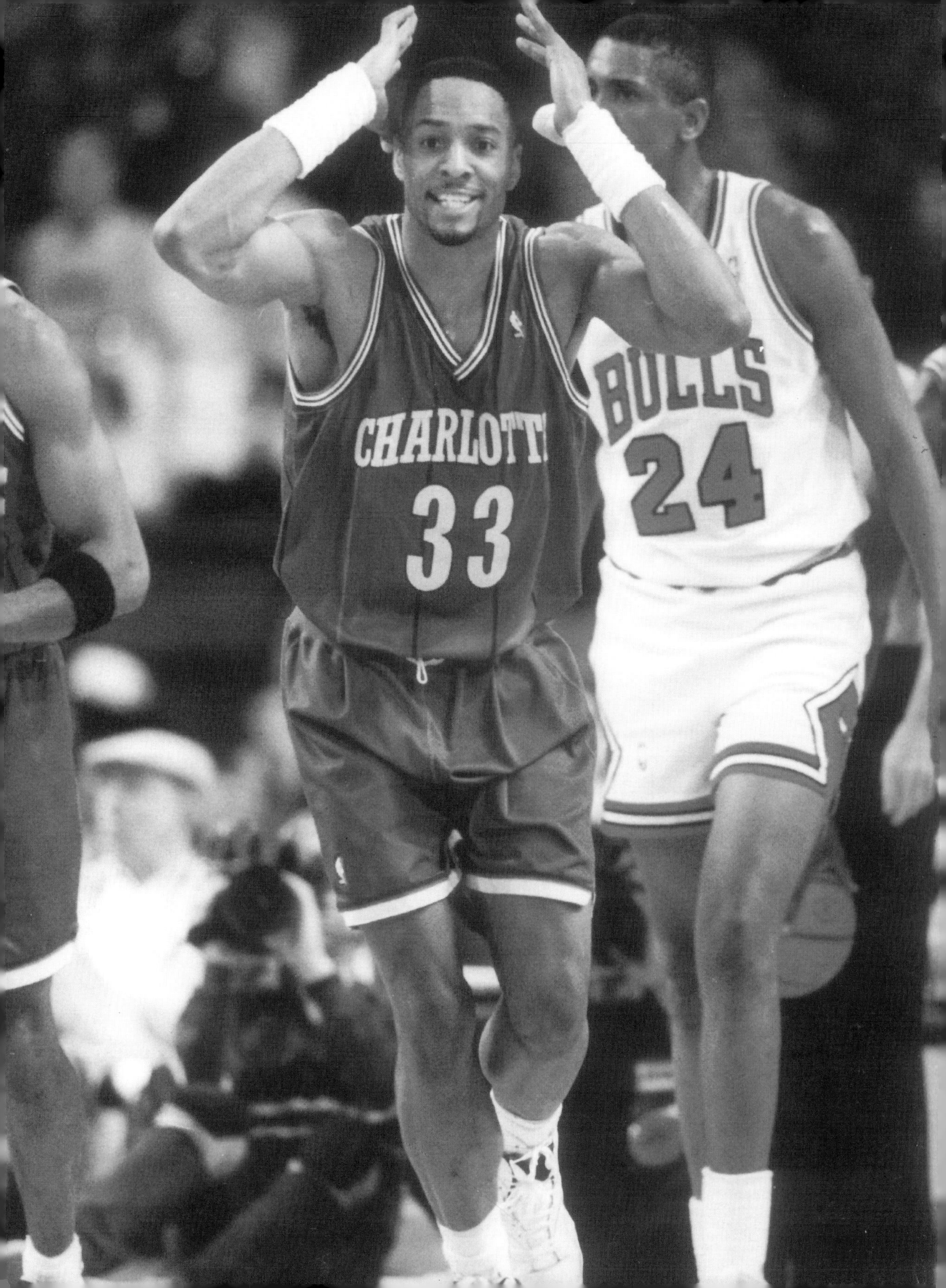
CHARLOTT
33
BULLS
24

1

A GREAT SHOT

With six seconds left to play in the game, Larry Johnson tried an eight-foot shot over Xavier McDaniel, but missed. The score was 103-102 in favor of the Boston Celtics, and the Charlotte Hornets seemed to be running out of miracles.

Robert Parish, the venerable Celtics center, battled for the rebound with Alonzo Mourning, the rookie center for the Hornets. The ball went out of bounds, last touched by Parish. There were 3.3 seconds left in the game. If Charlotte could score a field goal, they could oust the Celtics from the 1993 playoffs and move on to the second round.

It was little short of amazing that the Hornets were in this position. For their first four years, the Hornets were a team that aimed for mediocrity, and they struggled to reach even that level. They won only 20 games their first season, losing 62. They fell to a 19-63 record in their

Alonzo Mourning, celebrating a regular season victory over the Bulls, took the Charlotte Hornets to their first playoffs in 1993—his rookie year in the NBA.

sophomore year, and in year three, they made a few improvements to finish at 26-56. In their fourth season, Charlotte improved to a more respectable 31-51 record, thanks largely to the arrival of Larry Johnson, a burly 6-foot-7-inch forward from the University of Nevada-Las Vegas who was the 1991 College Player of the Year.

Now the Hornets were in the playoffs, and it was again a rookie addition who had made the biggest difference. In drafting Alonzo Mourning, Charlotte finally had the big man they had long desired. He was a player who was extremely focused on winning, a player who could score and rebound with vigor, a player who could complement Johnson up front, giving the team a powerful 1-2 offensive punch. With Mourning, the Hornets became winners, recording their first season in which they won more games than they lost, with a 44-38 record. With winning came the joy of a spot in the playoffs.

Charlotte's opponent was the Boston Celtics, the most glorified team in the history of the NBA. The proud Celtics, with such greats as Bill Russell, Bob Cousy, Larry Bird, Bill Sharman, and John Havlicek, had won 16 NBA championships, far more than any other team. While the Celtics had not won a title since 1986 and had won only 48 games in the 1992-93 season—only their second time under 50 wins in 14 years—they still were a feared and formidable team. Even though Bird had retired the previous season, they still had potential Hall of Famers in the gangling forward Kevin McHale, the exciting forward Reggie Lewis, who was their leading scorer, and 7-foot center Robert Parish. Parish, who would be the main man trying to stifle Mourning, already had five world championship rings.

The experts were predicting the Celtics would beat the Hornets. After all, Boston had won four more games than Charlotte and had finished in second place in the Atlantic Division while the Hornets were third in the Central Division. In addition, Boston had beaten them three games to one in head-to-head competition, and almost all of their players had playoff experience while few of the Charlotte players had any. On top of that, Boston had a legendary home-court advantage. Over the years, the Celtics had rarely lost an important playoff game on their renowned parquet floor at the fabled Boston Garden.

The Charlotte Hornets' Larry Johnson (2) and Tyrone Bogues hug each other during the final seconds of Charlotte's 99-98 double overtime win against the Celtics in Game 2 of the first round of the 1993 Eastern Conference playoffs.

Mourning had made his presence felt in each of the playoff games so far. He and Kendall Gill had scored a game-high 30 points in Game 1, although Boston won, 112-101. In Game 2, Mourning was Charlotte's leading rebounder, pulling down 14, as the Hornets outlasted the Celtics 99-98 in double overtime. The thrilling game was shown on NBC, marking the Hornets' first appearance on national television. The victory was exactly what the Hornets needed. No one on the team wanted to go back to Boston to play a sudden-death game in front of a crowd of excited Celtic fans.

If the Hornets wanted to move on in the play-offs, they had to win both Games 3 and 4 at home. They accomplished the first part of this task after they ran off a 15-0 spurt during the second period of Game 3 and wound up winning 119-89, handing the embarrassed and shell-shocked Celtics their third-worst loss in playoff history.

Now, the Hornets were only one victory away from clinching their first playoff series. Game 4 was played on May 5, 1993, before another jam-packed, foot-stomping, towel-waving, scream-ing crowd of 23,698 at the Charlotte Coliseum. At first, it appeared this game would be anoth-er rout, as Charlotte built an 18-point lead, 88-70, entering the fourth quarter. The advantage was 16 points with less than nine minutes to go, but Boston refused to quit. The Celtics shaved the lead to nine points with 3:21 remaining. Still, the arena known as The Hive was buzzing in anticipation of a glorious victory celebration.

The Celtics' veterans—Parish and McHale—suddenly launched a furious Boston comeback. After a field goal by guard Kevin Gamble, the Celtics trailed by only one, 102-101, with 1:06 left. When Sherman Douglas stripped Larry Johnson of the ball and scored on a driving layup with 42.7 seconds to go, the Celtics were ahead by one, and the Hornets and the crowd were stunned.

"We knew they had a tendency of giving up big leads all year," Celtics forward Xavier McDaniel said. "We just kept working on it."

After Douglas's go-ahead basket, the Hornets came down court and Gill missed a jumper that

Parish rebounded. With a chance to control the game, Boston turned the ball over on a terrible mistake by Rick Fox—a 10-second violation for failure to get across midcourt, and Charlotte regained possession with 21.9 seconds remaining. Fox could have called time out, but neglected to do so.

Larry Johnson's missed jumper with six seconds left could have been Charlotte's last hurrah, but Mourning got Parish to touch the ball last before it went out of bounds. The Hornets called time out and set up a play with 3.3 seconds left on the clock. Mourning had already scored a career playoff high of 31 points with six blocks, but he wasn't done for the evening. He was not going to pass up a chance to be the big man, the go-to guy, again for the Hornets.

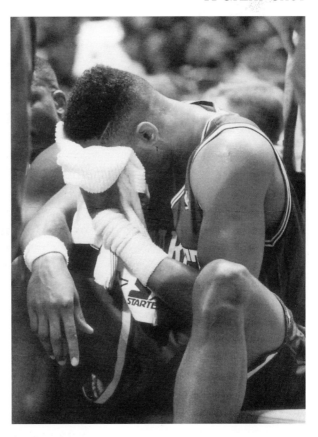

Mourning and the Hornets refused to throw in the towel when the Celtics took the lead with only 42 seconds left in Game 4 of the first round of the 1993 Eastern Conference playoffs.

On the inbounds play, Dell Curry got the ball and Mourning set a pick for Kendall Gill. Parish came over quickly to help, leaving Mourning wide open. Curry flipped the ball to Mourning, who dribbled once to his right, then fired a jumper from behind the foul line as McDaniel came lunging at him. Not many centers have a reliable shot from that far away from the basket, but Mourning does. The ball went cleanly through the net and the Charlotte players buried Mourning under a sea of bodies as he fell to the floor, raising both fists at first, then extending both arms.

A fan shook a banner that read "Zo's no rookie," using Mourning's nickname. For a rookie,

Mourning had shown tremendous composure under pressure.

Again, though, the Hornets' celebration was premature. The game wasn't over yet. While almost everyone thought that time had expired—the clock showed no time remaining—when Mourning made his dramatic shot, the officials said there still were four-tenths of a second left and ordered the clock reset.

Boston had time for one play—and one play only. After taking a time out to set it up, the Celtics inbounded the ball at midcourt. McHale took it out and tossed a perfect alley-oop pass toward Dee Brown. Brown has a 45-inch vertical leap, making him one of the best leapers in the league. Gill, who was defending Brown, jumped and appeared to block the shot from two feet away. The officials agreed that it was a block and said the game was over, triggering a celebration among the Charlotte players and fans. Brown didn't agree with the call, however, and protested vehemently. He claimed that Gill should have been called for goaltending.

"The ball was definitely in," an angry Brown insisted. "It was goaltending all the way. I laid the ball in the rim, so I know it was goaltending. It wasn't like a jump shot. Kendall definitely knocked the ball off the rim. You have to make that call, no matter how much time is left in the game, whatever the circumstances. If it wasn't goaltending, then I think there should have been a foul called."

If goaltending had been allowed, it would have made the Celtics the winner and sent the series back to Boston for a decisive fifth game.

"I just kept thinking, 'I don't want to go back to Boston,'" the Hornets' Kenny Gattison said.

He didn't have to worry. The officials upheld their original decision, disallowing Brown's protest, and the emotional game was officially over—a 104-103 victory for the spirited Hornets.

"It makes you feel good that you are a part of this first playoff appearance in the history of this organization," the ebullient Mourning said, after escaping from the clutches of his excited teammates.

"I don't think anything can compare to this. This is the greatest thrill of my basketball career. The only thing that compares to this is me getting the chance just to play the game of basketball. Me being blessed with this body, this mind, and these talents."

Mourning's clutch jumper that won the game was the same shot that used to frustrate his teammates and coaches. "We've been trying to get him to pass up that shot all year," point guard Muggsy Bogues said. "We've been trying to get him to swing the ball. But I'm glad he shot it this time."

So was everyone else in the Charlotte organization. Winning the series ended five years of frustration, five years of wondering if the Hornets ever would be able to compete with the league's elite teams.

Winning also triggered a party among the fans who spilled into the streets of Charlotte. But first fans spent 10 minutes in the Coliseum chanting, "Zo," and "We want New York," a reference to the Hornets' next series opponent, the Knicks.

"I gained a lot of respect for Mourning when he hit that shot," said Parish, who ironically would become Mourning's teammate at the start of the 1994-95 season when he signed with Char-

lotte after Boston released him. "He showed a lot of character and poise."

Mourning just called it "a lucky shot."

"Fortunately, the ball bounced our way," he added. "I could have missed that shot. But it went in, and we're going on."

Hornets coach Allan Bristow said, "We couldn't have scripted it any better. That was a great shot by Alonzo. Boston never gave up. We all knew they were going to come back. You know what? I sort of expected it. Once they got back into the game, we couldn't find our legs. We were playing not to lose. We got complacent. I'm just glad we had enough points to hang on to win. It's hard to hold a big lead, but the bottom line is we let it go and got it back. We won this game. We didn't get it as a gift."

The loss for the Celtics also marked the end of McHale's illustrious 13-year playing career. When the game was over, he announced his retirement. Several Hornets' players, including Mourning, hugged him.

It was some ending, both for McHale and Mourning.

"Nobody who was here is ever going to forget this game and this series," Gattison said.

The city of Charlotte expressed its appreciation for Mourning with this 21,000 square-foot mural in the downtown area.

2

GROWING UP

Alonzo Mourning was born on February 8, 1970. Peace was rare in his house because his father, Alonzo Sr., who worked at the shipyards, and his mother, Julia, were constantly arguing and fighting. Alonzo felt torn because he didn't want to take sides.

When he was 10, his parents split up. They got back together the next year and had a daughter. But when Alonzo was 12, they separated again. This time, they placed him with a friend of the family, Fannie Threet, a retired schoolteacher and a very religious woman. Mrs. Threet specialized in working with children who needed care. She and her husband had taken care of about 50 children.

With Mrs. Threet and her husband, Mourning had to adjust to a new home and a new way of life. It was not easy. "I think certain parts of it were headaches and certain parts were very

Alonzo Mourning, here playing for his college team, the Georgetown Hoyas, was a natural basketball player because of his height and agility.

joyful," he said. "No part of life is always going to be milk and cookies."

Mourning was always taller than the other kids his age at the foster home. "When I was sort of hanging over the bed," he said, Mrs. Threet found him a mattress two feet longer than his old one.

"I'm not saying Alonzo was a perfect child," Mrs. Threet said. "But he always was obedient. And he was a hungry child. For breakfast, one box of Cap'n Crunch wouldn't do. You'd have to give him two or three of the larger ones."

Mourning's height made him a natural for basketball, but he was awkward, like many youngsters his size. "When I was 12 or 13, a lot of people doubted me," he said. "They didn't think I could succeed. When I was trying to learn the game, people laughed at me because I was tall and skinny and clumsy. I was goofy. I was a stiff. Those people that doubted me didn't realize they were giving me extra incentive to succeed."

That incentive helped Mourning develop into a graceful and fluid player, and he became a star at Indian River High School in Chesapeake, Virginia. He was such an outstanding player, especially as a shot-blocker, that he was heavily recruited by several colleges. Bob Gibbons, a college recruiting guru, ranked Mourning as the number one high school senior in 1988. That helped make Mourning the country's most highly recruited high school player.

Enhancing his reputation even more was an invitation to the 1988 Olympic trials before Mourning played a minute of college basketball.

He was the first high school student ever to be invited to the trials, and he played well in the practices. Performing against the game's

best collegians—most of whom would enter the pros later that year—he showed what he could do. During the trials, he and his teammates also scrimmaged against a group of NBA players, including Patrick Ewing, in a series of exhibition games and survived until the final cut.

"Trying out for the Olympics and playing against all that talent really molded me to the point where I was ready," Mourning said. "I knew I would be comfortable in the college atmosphere, so I didn't have to all of a sudden adjust to it. Just by playing against that talent, I learned."

Mourning didn't mind all the attention he

Mourning was the first high school student ever to be invited to the Olympic trials, enhancing his recruitment by college teams across the country. Georgetown was his top choice.

Mourning admired Patrick Ewing when he watched the 1982 NCAA championship game. Ewing, shown here in a 1982 game against Wisconsin, was a dominating player in his freshman year.

received—from journalists as well as college recruiters. "It enables kids to get into position to go to a good college," he said.

Checking out colleges was a memorable experience for Mourning. At Georgia Tech, he met singer Anita Baker. At Virginia, the daughter of then-coach Terry Holland introduced him to her pet snake.

Mourning opted for Georgetown, mainly because of Patrick Ewing and Coach John Thompson. Ewing had attended the school and was an All-America player before going on to become the number-one pick in the 1985 NBA draft by the New York Knicks.

While growing up and living fairly close to Georgetown, Mourning first saw Ewing play in the NCAA championship game in 1982 when Ewing was a freshman. Mourning was enamored of his work ethic and his intensity.

"I just wanted to go out on the court the next day and play that way," he said. "He really just made it work for me. He sparked the vibe."

Mourning first met Ewing when he played at a basketball camp at Princeton University when he was 15 or 16. Ewing was sitting in the stands at Jadwin Gymnasium talking with Thompson, then came down to the court to greet Mourning and chat briefly. "I was stretching, and he tapped me on the shoulder and introduced himself to me and I shook his hand," Mourning said. "I was in awe."

The meeting was brief, but Mourning began following Ewing's career after that. So when it came time for Mourning to choose a college, he decided to go to Georgetown. Not only did he want to emulate Ewing, he admired Thompson "because of his values, the way he teaches, and the things he stands for."

Mourning was proud when he packed for Georgetown. No one in his family—not his grandparents, not his parents, and none of his 12 aunts and uncles—had gone to college. Alonzo carried all their good wishes with him.

3

AT GEORGETOWN

When Mourning entered Georgetown in 1988, he was hailed as the next Patrick Ewing, a player who would lead the Hoyas to a national championship. There were other comparisons, too.

He was already being compared to former collegiate greats such as Lew Alcindor (who later changed his name to Kareem Abdul-Jabbar), Bill Walton, Sam Bowie, and Ralph Sampson. There were also comparisons to Moses Malone and Darryl Dawkins, both of whom went directly from high school into the pros. Many felt the young Mourning was ready to step right into the NBA, skipping college completely. Mourning was going to be the game's next superstar. The pressure was enormous, the expectations gargantuan.

Still, he was so young, he couldn't quite com-

Mourning, shown here blocking a shot against N.C. State in the 1989 NCAA Eastern Regional playoffs, had a very successful freshman season at Georgetown even though the Hoyas did not make it to the top of the NCAA.

prehend the prophecies that were being laid down for him and the difficulty he would have in fulfilling them. Thompson tried to smooth the way for the young phenom.

"With the kind of publicity that Alonzo had, no kid can possibly be what his accolades are when he comes out of high school," Thompson said. "It's a burden that he will have to bear. I think he will have to evaluate what's going on as to what's perceived about him. He's been conditioned to be Alonzo all his life since he was able to play basketball, and the coming of the savior—that label was hung on him. I think he's become accustomed to it."

Thompson said the expectations would not go away in Mourning's four years at Georgetown. He advised Mourning to keep his composure and not worry about what other people thought, and he would be fine.

Mourning also tried to take the pressure off himself. "I think the expectations are something that I've gone beyond," he said. "If I worried constantly about that, I'd get caught up in what people expected of me and not be able to play my game. So I can put that aside and go out and play as hard as I can. Basically, that's all I can give somebody who pays for a ticket to see me play."

When Mourning finally arrived at Georgetown, the hype was overwhelming. His every move was going to be scrutinized and dissected. No matter how well he played, there always would be critics who would say he wasn't living up to his potential. He had to win a championship or else he would be a flop, some said.

Mourning relished the attention. He didn't enjoy the comparisons.

"All these comparisons create a little more pressure," he said, "but I shouldn't let them get to me because I'm not Patrick Ewing or anyone else. I'm Alonzo Mourning. What I have to do is work hard and play my game, work to reach my goals and make a name for myself."

While trying to establish his own identity, Mourning was going to do it with Ewing's number. He was given uniform number 33, the first Georgetown player to wear it since Ewing left in 1984.

Mourning didn't waste any time making a strong impression, quickly putting his name into the Georgetown record books. In the Hoyas' first home game of the 1988-89 season, he registered the school's first "triple-double" with 11 points, 10 rebounds, and a Georgetown-record 11 blocked shots against St. Leo.

Mourning passes under the arms of Pittsburgh's Brian Shorter, left, and Darelle Porter in the 1989 Big East Finals.

A short time later, Mourning blitzed Miami for 26 points and 17 rebounds, prompting Hurricanes coach Bill Foster to say, "There's no question that since Moses [Malone], he's the best big kid to come out of high school."

After Mourning scored 15 points and blocked seven shots against the University of Pittsburgh early in 1989, Panthers coach Paul Evans remarked, "I said last year that if I was owner of one of the seven teams in the NBA lottery, I would have gotten Mourning out of high school. Two years down the road, he's better than the

Duke guard Grant Hill, left, looks to pass around the defense of Mourning. Alonzo was chosen 1989 Big East Conference Defensive Player of the year during his freshman year at Georgetown.

kids that went in the lottery last year. The kid loves to play defense as much as offense. You just don't see that kind of defensive intensity in a kid coming out of high school."

Dwayne Schintzius, Florida's 7-foot-2-inch center, couldn't believe Mourning was only a freshman. "A freshman?" Schintzius said. "He's more like an early junior. I just wish I had his physical attributes when I was coming out of high school. I was scared to take the ball to the basket then. But this guy will take the ball to the hole and knock your teeth out."

Mourning didn't take the Hoyas to the NCAA championship as a freshman, but under the circumstances he had a very rewarding season. He showed that he was a fine offensive player with his wide variety of shots and range. He also proved that he was a superior shot-blocker by setting the school record for blocks. "I don't go out and look for blocked shots," Mourning said. "If it's there, I go get it." He led the nation in blocked shots with a school-record 169, an average of 4.97 per game. He was Georgetown's top rebounder with an average of 7.3 per game and second-leading scorer with a 13.2 average. He was chosen the Big East Conference Defensive Player of the Year and a third-team All-American, and he was the driving force behind Georgetown's 29-5 record, its winning the Big East regular-season title, and the conference tournament. The Hoyas then lost to Duke and its less-heralded freshman, Christian Laettner, in the NCAA East Regional final.

"He made some freshman mistakes, but I think it would be weird if in his freshman year, he didn't," Thompson said. "We have to remember that with all of the accolades and comparisons we go through with Alonzo, he's still a freshman."

Thompson was content to bring his prodigy along slowly. "I don't want somebody to come in here at 18, 19 years old and become a super-human being," he said. "He's got to go through a maturation period. So if he makes some mistakes, it's a good thing, because it gives me a chance to teach."

Despite his productive season, Mourning wasn't fully pleased. He was hungry to find ways to improve. "I have to work on all parts of my game," he said. "I'm never satisfied, because there's always room for improvement. Even if I was the best player in the world, I'd still have a lot of things to learn."

One thing he learned was not to associate with the wrong people. During the off-season, he was discovered to have fraternized with alleged drug kingpin Rayful Edmond III. Mourning admitted his mistake and said he would make sure to be more careful in the future.

"It hurt me," he said, "but that's something I can use for the rest of my life, learning about who I associate with, because I'm going to be introduced to so many people while doing what I do right now."

The maturation of Mourning continued in his sophomore season. After his freshman year, he worked on developing a short left-handed hook shot to complement the assortment of

Georgetown's coach, John Thompson, was a tremendous influence on Mourning. A true mentor, he was one of the main reasons Alonzo chose Georgetown.

shots he had with his right hand. He also lifted weights with 7-foot-2-inch junior center Dikembe Mutombo.

A few years before, Coach Guy Lewis of the University of Houston had given a scholarship to a tall athletic Nigerian, even though the kid had never been to America and had only played basketball for a few years. But Hakeem Olajuwon had turned out to be a gem, learning basketball skills quickly and taking his college team to the NCAA finals. He then went on to a stellar NBA career.

Coach John Thompson felt he might have another version of Hakeem Olajuwon in Dikembe Mutombo. Mutombo, from Zaire, was taller than either Olajuwon or Mourning and reputedly spoke seven languages. While he lacked Mourning's grace and touch, he was an even more devastating shot-blocker.

Mutombo was a junior during the 1989-90 season, and he had played little in the years before as Thompson tried to teach him the game. But now Thompson figured he needed to showcase Mutombo for his last two seasons, and he placed the big man in the middle, asking Mourning to switch to power forward.

Some big men have done well by moving to power forward. The tall but skinny Ralph Sampson benefited from not being banged around so much. But while with the Knicks, Patrick Ewing had been asked to make the switch in favor of Bill Cartwright at center, and the move made everyone unhappy.

No doubt, the switch diminished Mourning's effectiveness. He had to learn a different offensive and defensive mindset. Although Mourning's scoring average increased to 16.5 per game, his rebound average rose to 8.5, and he was selected a second-team All-America player, his numbers over the second half of the season were not as good as those during the first half. He finished with only 69 blocks, 100 fewer than his freshman year.

Marring the season was a distasteful anti-Semitic remark Mourning reportedly made to Connecticut's Israeli star Nadav Henefeld. Capping the year was an early tournament loss to Xavier of Ohio, as Mourning was rendered ineffective by two Musketeers and future pros—Tyrone Hill and Derek Strong.

Mourning's junior season was worse than his sophomore year. Thompson decided from the beginning to make Mutombo a full-time player, keeping Mourning at his unnatural and uncomfortable position of power forward—facing the basket. Mutombo had taken over the marquee position of center and Mourning was unhappy. Mutombo was blocking the shots and getting the rebounds, and Mourning was relegated to a secondary role.

A strained arch in Mourning's left foot didn't help. He had sustained the injury while playing with U.S. teams in the Goodwill Games and World Championships during the summer of 1990. He reinjured the arch during an early season victory over Duke, then missed nine games and parts of several others.

As center for the Georgetown Hoyas, Mourning preferred playing defense. Here he dominates the net against St. John's in the 1992 Big East Tournament.

Being forced to play power forward was frustrating for Mourning, and being unable to play at all was more aggravating. When he was healthy, he tried to make the combination of Mourning and Mutombo—the M&M boys—work in the Georgetown front court. But the chemistry was all wrong. "What am I supposed to do, fight Dikembe for the ball?" Mourning said.

Other teams realized the Hoyas' dilemma and took advantage. With Mourning and Mutombo in the lineup at the same time, the lane often got clogged up, and confusion reigned on offense for Georgetown. Mourning, accustomed to playing in the middle, often drifted into the paint area, where there was little room for both him and Mutombo to maneuver. Mourning was out of position and out of sync.

"I've played basketball over 10 or 11 years now, and I know I'm capable of playing this game," he said. "I don't think I've ever been in a slump like I am now. I know I'm capable of playing better, but it's just not working out for me."

When the season ended, Mourning's scoring average had slipped to 15.8 and his rebound average had fallen to 7.7. Georgetown's record was a mediocre 19-13, and the Hoyas were beaten in the second round of the NCAA tournament.

Much to Mourning's credit, he did not make excuses—not the switch to power forward, not the foot injury. "The ball just wasn't going in the basket for me," he said simply.

Thompson blamed Mourning's decline on a psychological problem. "Zo tried to do everything we asked him to do," the coach said. "He worked hard, but he got to a point where he got so uptight about things when they went wrong."

Thompson, however, was confident that Mourning would return to his old form in his senior season. "He'll work through this," he said. "Next year, for certain, he'll be free."

Free because Mutombo had graduated and gone on to the pros, drafted in the first round— number four overall—by the Denver Nuggets. That enabled Mourning to return to center, the position where he felt most comfortable.

Mourning also could have chosen to declare himself eligible for the NBA draft after his junior year. Instead, he decided to complete his college education and earn his degree in sociology. Since he was the first from his family to attend college, he wanted to be the first to finish.

"The money is always going to be there," Mourning said. "But I'm not in a rush. I'm concentrating on my degree. That's one of my basic goals in life. And it's one of the things my mother would really want."

He also felt he needed to mature more. "I told him I thought he was correct," Thompson said.

Based on his junior season, Mourning also thought people would have doubts about his ability to make it in the NBA, and he wanted to prove them wrong.

"It was much better for me to stay," Mourning said. "I think I did the right thing."

Mourning did not resent his coach for moving him to power forward and letting Mutombo take his starting center spot. "Coach Thompson was somewhat of a father figure," Mourning said. "My own father thanked him at my graduation [from Georgetown]. My father told him when I wasn't there, you were there. I can respect my father for saying that. It's not like my father was saying that he didn't do his job. It takes a man to thank another man, and I realize the influence that Coach Thompson has had on me."

Now starting again in the middle, Mourning felt like a young thoroughbred just turned loose on the racetrack. He was free to roam under the basket again. Free to be the dominating center he had been in years past. "I prefer to play center," he said. "I'm more effective closer to the basket. I can contribute more overall to my team that way."

Contribute he did. Playing with his old fire and fury, Mourning set career highs in scoring average (21.7), and rebound average (10.7), and he was second in the nation behind Shaquille O'Neal of Louisiana State in blocked shots with 160. He also was the first player picked as Big East Player of the Year, Defensive Player of the Year, and Big East Tournament MVP in the same season. Topping the honors was his selection as a first team All-America player.

"I think Mourning is the true picture of an All-America," former St. John's coach Lou Carnesecca said. "His shot selection, control of himself, passing the ball, rebounding, playing good defense—he's the epitome."

One St. John's player agreed. "He's a problem," said Malik Sealy. "He takes up so much space. You have to know where he is on the court."

The NBA scouts also were watching Mourning carefully, and they were duly impressed. "He has the rare ability that when he blocks a shot,

In his senior year, Mourning became the dominating center of the Big East and was again named Defensive Player of the Year in 1992.

Mourning is greeted by NBA Commissioner David Stern after being picked in the 1992 NBA Draft by the Charlotte Hornets.

he keeps it in play," scout Walt Ferrin of the Minnesota Timberwolves said. "Most guys try to put it in the upper balcony."

Shot-blocking was the strongest part of Mourning's game. He blocked 27 shots in a national AAU game and 21 against a touring Soviet Union team.

Mourning finished his career as the second player in Georgetown history (along with Ewing) to collect more than 2,000 points (2,001) and 1,000 rebounds (1,032). He also ranked second behind Ewing in career blocked shots with 453 and was the Hoyas' all-time leader in free throws made (771) and free throws attempted (1,023).

Mourning's final game for Georgetown in Madison Square Garden—the mecca of college basketball—was a 56-54 loss to Syracuse in the Big East tournament. Ewing stood in the Hoyas' locker room.

"Good luck," Ewing yelled.

"All right," Mourning said.

Now Mourning was ready for the pros. He had reestablished his greatness. And the NBA was waiting for him with open arms and open checkbooks.

Mourning's two main rivals at the top of the wish list for teams with draft picks were Shaquille O'Neal and Christian Laettner. Laettner, a 6-foot-10-inch center/forward led a powerful Duke team to two national championships and was the sole collegiate representative on the Dream Team, which won a gold medal at the 1988 Olympics. O'Neal had never gotten his LSU Tigers far in the NCAA playoffs, but at 7-feet-1-inch and 300 pounds, he was as amazingly athletic as he was amazingly large.

O'Neal made himself available for the draft although he was only a junior, and the Orlando Magic did not hesitate to choose him first. The Charlotte Hornets, a team that had floundered in its first four years of existence, were only too happy to take Mourning, a dominating player under the basket. Laettner went third, to Minnesota.

4

WITH THE HORNETS

The pressure was on Mourning to produce in his first year in the pros, and produce quickly, just like during his freshman year at Georgetown. The Hornets wanted desperately to appease the loyal and faithful fans who had been filling the Charlotte Coliseum by rewarding them with a team capable of making the NBA playoffs. The Hornets had played like a sick team for four years, and now it was Mourning's responsibility to provide a cure.

Marty Blake, the NBA's director of scouting, was certain that Mourning would be the Hornets' elixir. "I think Mourning is the type of guy who will be much better as a pro," Blake said. "He can score and he's very determined. I have no qualms about Alonzo. He's going to be an outstanding pro."

Georgetown coach John Thompson couldn't wait to see his prodigy in the pros. "It was very hard for him to be creative [in college], because

Wearing #33, Alonzo Mourning first put on the Charlotte Hornets' uniform in 1993.

Mourning's play impressed many NBA coaches and players. An intense player, he reached for the heights in every game.

teams kept sagging three or four men back on him," Thompson said. "When he gets to the next level, he'll have more freedom to operate."

And Mourning had more freedom, because in the NBA, zone defenses were illegal. Man-to-man defenses were the norm, so there was little sagging on the centers. Another factor was that in the pros most every player was considered a good shooter, so dropping off a man to help a teammate on defense made little sense, since getting the ball to a wide open player would be almost a sure two— or three—points.

That was the way Mourning liked it. Despite his NBA inexperience, he felt he had the speed, the quickness, the jumping ability, and the agility to compete with the league's best centers. Just give him the ball and give him some space. He would not be intimidated.

"Intimidation is just a word," Mourning said. "I look at it this way: I played against Patrick Ewing and Dikembe Mutombo for four summers straight in college, and I'm thinking, 'If I can play against those guys, I can play against anybody who steps on the floor.' So intimidation? That's not even in my vocabulary."

First Mourning played hardball with the man-

agement of the Hornets. When his contract negotiations went slowly, Mourning held out and
missed all of training camp. Not until after the
first four games of the regular season did he finally sign the six-year contract worth between $25
million and $26.25 million. Coach Allan Bristow
was relieved when the deal was finalized. He said,
"He gives us presence. Teams shot close to 50
percent against us last year. You won't go any-
where in the NBA allowing that kind of shooting."

Mourning used some of his money to buy a
house for each of his parents—and one for Mrs.
Threet. "I'm excited," Mourning said. "Now I can
concentrate on what I do best, and that's playing basketball."

His NBA debut finally came in a 110-109 loss
to the Pacers in Indiana. Wearing his familiar
number 33 jersey, he took Charlotte's first shot,
a left-handed hook that careened off the glass,
then scored the Hornets' first basket on a 15-
foot jumper. He finished with 12 points, three
rebounds, and one blocked shot, in a performance limited to 19 minutes because of foul
trouble. Mourning had arrived—impressively,
even if briefly.

"If it wasn't for him, we wouldn't even have
been in the game," said teammate Larry Johnson, the top pick in the 1991 draft and the 1991-
92 Rookie of the Year. "He helped us more than
he hurt us. . . . He's going to be a great player.
He stepped right in and got right into it."

Guard Muggsy Bogues, the NBA's smallest
player at 5'3", also was an immediate believer in
the towering rookie center who dwarfed him like
Goliath did David. "Once he learns the NBA game,
he's going to be difficult to stop," Bogues said.

It didn't take long for Mourning to learn the

NBA game. In the Hornets' first 33 games with Mourning, they were 17-16, compared with 9-24 the previous season. During that time, Mourning set franchise records for blocked shots in a game (7) and a season (108).

"He has the whole package," Detroit Pistons coach Ron Rothstein said. "He runs, jumps, scores, plays hard, blocks shots, and defenses well."

Even more impressed was the New York Knicks' rock-solid, outspoken forward Anthony Mason. "He's got a much more all-around game than Shaq," Mason said of Mourning, comparing him to the other rookie making headlines. "I'm sure Shaq is going to be a great player in this league, but as far as Shaq is concerned right now, he can't touch Alonzo. You don't have to worry about him going out there and shooting the jumper or driving around you. He never goes to the basket weak, and even if he misses, he always follows his shot. There's nothing Alonzo can't do."

Mourning showed an extraordinary passion to win. Sometimes, though, he let his emotions get the best of him, detracting from his play. Too often, he argued with officials over foul calls, and his rash actions cost him technical fouls and ejections. In his first season with the Hornets, he drew 16 technicals and two ejections.

Mourning was fined $5,000 for a fight with Detroit's troublesome center, Bill Laimbeer, in his rookie season. After the two were ejected, Mourning strode toward the Pistons' locker room, apparently wanting to continue the scuffle, and had to be physically restrained. He didn't realize how he had played into Laimbeer's hands. One of the head goons on a team that had earned two NBA championship rings and whose players were known as "the Bad Boys," Laimbeer specialized in taunting his team's leading opposition. Laimbeer's trash talk, and sometimes hyperactive elbows, had gotten him thrown out of several games—but if he took his opponents' best player with him, he figured it was a way of helping his own team.

Mourning, who never was thrown out of a game until he entered the NBA, committed his worst offense in November 1994. He was fined $5,000 after a loss at Boston where he berated referee Steve Javie at midcourt and repeatedly criticized the officiating crew after the game.

The officials then cited him in an anonymous survey as one of the league's biggest complainers.

Mourning was also hit with 24 technicals and ejected five times in his sophomore year in the NBA. "I just let my emotions go my first two seasons," Mourning said. "They dictated whatever I did."

After that, he learned to curb his temper. Some wise words of advice from the NBA's elder statesman at the time, Robert Parish, helped calm down Mourning. Parish had played four seasons with Golden State and 14 with Boston before joining the Hornets for the 1994-95 season. Parish talked to the youthful Mourning about self-control.

"In training camp, I commented on one area he needed to clean up—he couldn't lose his concentration," Parish said. "He needed to learn that you have to put the brakes on sometimes. Or, if

Mourning out-maneuvers Detroit Piston Greg Anderson in a March 1994 game. Mourning's play improved in his third season with the Hornets after coaching from fellow teammate Robert Parish.

you're incapable of putting the brakes on, you don't get yourself into that situation."

Parish's influence worked. In his third season, Mourning was tagged with only seven technicals and wasn't ejected from a single game. Staying in the game made him more effective, said Parish, "because he focuses his energy on the court rather than on an official or a fan."

To prove how well Mourning had cleaned up his act, he apologized on court to Charles Barkley after a bumping incident when Sir Charles was the star of the Phoenix Suns. That's not something he would have done as a rookie.

That same season, Mourning was banged into the basket support by Seattle's Sam Perkins on a drive to the hoop. In the past, Mourning would have grown infuriated and vented his anger at Perkins after the hard foul, which was ruled flagrant, and likely would have gotten tossed out of the game. Instead, he remained calm, the Hornets kept the ball, and eventually they won the game.

"That was a great example of Zo turning the other cheek," Coach Bristow said.

Despite his mellowness under trying conditions, Mourning did not lose his intensity or his passion for the game. His will to win never wavered. "I don't care if we're playing Miami Beach Elementary School, I'm going to play hard," he said. "I want to win 82 games."

LeRon Ellis, a Charlotte teammate, was keenly aware of the burning desire in Mourning. "When you play with Zo, whatever intensity level you're on, it goes up," Ellis said. "He does it in practice, too. He works hard all the time."

Echoing Ellis was George Raveling, a well-traveled college coach and a well-known coach of U.S. national teams. "The thing you have to like about Alonzo is he's going to work to get better," Raveling said. "He's a warrior that way. If you pay him a buck-fifty an hour, he'll give you two bucks worth of work. He'll always give you more than you ask for."

Mourning felt he had to work extra hard because he was a center, not a very glamorous position the way he described it—more like a sewer cleaner. "The position I play is very aggressive—elbows flying, people pushing, barking; you're all up in people's face, smelling people's breath," he said. "It's not too pleasant down there in the hole. That's why only a select few play down there. A lot of people get paid big bucks [in the NBA], but very rarely do you find people that want to go down there and put up with that night in and night out. I'm one of the select few who likes to do it."

A quick learner, Mourning rapidly picked up the nuances of the game and proved to be a major handful for opposing centers. "I have to be smart," he said. "This game is just like a chess game. When someone takes a move at you, you have to go to the next step. And basically, that's all collapsing back on the post is. They take away your moves inside, so you burn them with hitting the open man.

"The sky's the limit of my potential, if I continue to have the same mind-set—playing hard and always thinking there is someone better than me."

He tried to pattern his game after that of Bill Russell, the Hall of Fame center who helped the Boston Celtics dominate the NBA from the mid-1950s to the late 1960s. Mourning learned about Russell from John Thompson—and Thompson learned about Russell by playing backup for him for three years on the world championship Boston Celtics.

"He always said, 'Bill Russell never led the NBA in scoring or anything like that, but he has more championship rings [11] than he has fingers,' " Mourning quoted Thompson as saying. "Regardless of how many points are scored, people will always remember how many championships you have won. That is what will go down in history. Whoever wins, that's what counts."

Before winning a title, though, the Hornets had to get to the postseason. In Mourning, they believed they had the player to lead them to the promised NBA after-season. They were correct.

On April 21, 1993, the Hornets clinched their first playoff berth by defeating the Milwaukee Bucks 119-111 before a raucous capacity crowd of 23,698 at the Charlotte Coliseum. The victory was the third in a five-game winning streak that closed the season for Charlotte and enabled the Hornets to finish with a 44-38 record—a significant 13-game improvement over 1991-92. What a difference Mourning had made.

Mourning's rookie season included a 21.0 scoring average, 10.3 rebounding average, and a club-record 271 blocks in 78 games (he missed only the four games in which he was a holdout).

In the first round of the playoffs, the Hornets were matched against the proud Celtics. After losing the first game, the Hornets reeled off three straight victories to win the best-of-five series. Mourning was a major force in Charlotte's first playoff win, 99-98 in double overtime, with 18 points, 14 rebounds, and six blocks before fouling out. He was the hero of the clinching 104-103 fourth-game victory with his 20-foot jumper with four-tenths of a second remaining. He finished Game 4 with 33 points and six blocks.

Four days after eliminating the Celtics, the Hornets opened Round 2 of the playoffs against the New York Knicks, a team Charlotte had lost three of four against during the regular season. The series saw the fascinating matchup of teacher versus pupil: Ewing versus Mourning. While the Knicks were clearly a better team, Mourning opened people's eyes as to who the better center might be.

In Game 1, a 111-95 New York victory, Mourning scored 27 points, grabbed 13 rebounds, and had four blocks. In New York's 105-101 overtime win in Game 2, Mourning led the Hornets with 24 points. Mourning put on a brilliant show in Game 3, scoring 34 points in Charlotte's 110-106 victory in double overtime. Game 4 was his only poor performance; he was held to 12 points and eight rebounds. In the finale, a 105-101 Knicks triumph, Mourning had 22 points and 12 rebounds.

A memorable first pro season had ended in defeat, but Mourning had nothing to be ashamed of. He had proven he could play in the NBA and that he could match up extremely well against the league's top centers.

"With Alonzo, we have three players who are capable of bringing us to a championship level,"

The Hornets' Alonzo Mourning faced his college idol, Patrick Ewing, in the second round of the 1993 NBA playoffs against the New York Knicks.

teammate Kendall Gill said, including himself, Mourning, and Larry Johnson, who all were under 25 at the time.

Mourning's second season was not nearly as memorable. Although he led the Hornets in scoring (21.5), rebounding (10.2), and blocks (3.13), Mourning missed 22 games because of injuries. The Hornets failed to make the playoffs, finishing with a 41-41 record. Between December 27, 1993, and March 11, 1994, Mourning and the team's other big scorer, Larry Johnson, who also was injured, were never in the lineup together, wiping out the Hornets' quest for consistency and teamwork, two of the major ingredients for a winning team. That season, Mourning's only consolation was being selected to play in the All-Star game, enhancing his status as one of the league's best players. He could not participate, however, because of his injuries.

While not all NBA players deserve to be looked upon as role models, Alonzo Mourning is one who fully merits the adoration he gets from kids. Although he is a very intense player on the court and disliked by some officials for his argumentative nature, he is a model of decorum off the field of play. Beneath the tough exterior is a gentle soul.

"There's Alonzo Mourning the basketball player and Alonzo Mourning the person, and I never bring them together," he said.

Mourning is very sensitive and caring about children because of the difficulties he encountered as a child. In Charlotte, he was captain of the NBA's 25-member Healthy Families, a program designed to generate awareness and funding for the prevention of child abuse. He also befriended a group of kids from the Thompson Children's Home, a residential treatment facility for abused children. Given his own tough childhood, he could identify with the youngsters there.

"I'm not saying I went through what these kids are going through," he said, "but I experienced some of the same problems. I want to make a difference. I tell the kids to keep their heads up and use what has happened to them as incentive. That's what I did.

"I love children more than adults. It's amazing how some kids listen to me more than to their own parents. I'll always try to help a child if I can. Every child deserves a home where they know love, not fear."

The 1994-95 season was a more pleasant experience for Mourning. Although his numbers were down slightly from the previous year, he averaged 21.3 points, 9.9 rebounds, and 2.92 blocks and had a .519 field goal percentage, making him only one of four players in the NBA to lead his team in four major statistical categories. The Hornets finished with their best record in history (50-32) and were back in the playoffs. In addition, Mourning was selected for the All-Star game again, and this time he was able to play, scoring 10 points and grabbing a team-high eight rebounds for the East in a 139-112 loss to the West.

Again, Mourning had a fine playoff series. Although the Hornets were beaten 3-1 by the Chicago Bulls in the opening round, Mourning averaged 22.0 points, 13.3 rebounds, and 3.25 blocks per game. Little did he realize that Game 4 against the Bulls, in which he scored 20 points and pulled down 13 rebounds, would be his last in a Charlotte uniform.

5

THE HEAT

Mourning had helped the Hornets shed their lowly expansion status. He had made them a legitimate team, a team capable of winning 50 games, and a team to be reckoned with. He had done it with passion and with his enormous will to win. He had done it by being a team player.

"I don't like to get involved in individual accomplishments," he said. "My mind is team-oriented. I understand the importance of doing the things to help a team win. . . . All I'm concerned with is winning. A lot of individual accomplishments only make one person happy, but when a team wins, that makes everybody excited."

Mourning had excited the people of Charlotte and everybody involved in the organization with his play during his first three seasons in the NBA. He had one more year remaining on his contract that would pay him $4.35 million for the 1995-96 season. After that, if the Hornets did not re-sign him, he would be a free agent.

After an opening-day trade, the 1995-96 season found Alonzo Mourning playing for the Miami Heat and working with Coach Pat Riley.

Mourning wanted to remain in Charlotte. He had become attached to the city. He had come from "a homey, Southern-type atmosphere," and since Charlotte fit that mold, he felt he fit in there. He liked Charlotte, and Charlotte liked him.

Looks, however, were deceiving. As much as Mourning was enjoying himself in Charlotte, professional basketball was a business, and he had to treat it as such. Appealing as the city was, Mourning felt a distaste for Hornets owner George Shinn. Mourning wanted to negotiate a contract extension prior to the season so he would not have to worry about it while playing. He claimed that Shinn told him the team "couldn't afford to pay me my fair market value."

What was Mourning's fair market value? He was offered an 11-year $100 million deal by the Hornets during the 1994-95 season and rejected it. He also rejected a seven-year $70 million offer from Charlotte after the season. Then, just before the 1995-96 season, he rejected another offer, this time for $11.2 million per season.

"He had no interest in it," Shinn said sadly. "He said, 'No, you've got to get closer to my money.' And it just broke my heart."

"I was willing to cooperate just as much as he was, because I wanted to be somewhere where I was going to be happy—somewhere I could prosper and win and be able to spend the rest of my career," Mourning said.

That somewhere was not going to be Charlotte. Reportedly, Mourning wanted $13 million per season, and the Hornets were not going to

Alonzo guards the net against Patrick Ewing in a Heats vs. Knicks game, April 1996.

pay that kind of outrageous sum to a player who had not yet won an individual or team title. The two sides were at loggerheads.

The Hornets could not pacify Mourning financially, and they knew that if he played for the team during the 1995-96 season it would be with a total lack of enthusiasm. So they tried working out a trade. Immediately, there was a huge amount of interest. The Los Angeles Lakers, Portland Trail Blazers, Atlanta Hawks, Miami Heat, Chicago Bulls, and Boston Celtics all were among Mourning's suitors. When Mourning learned that the deal would be with Miami and involve swingman Glen Rice going from the Heat to the Hornets, he also rejected that, saying the team would be too weak without the high-scoring Rice.

Finally, on opening day of the 1995-96 season, the trade with Miami was completed. Mourning went to the Heat, along with guard Pete Myers and center-forward LeRon Ellis. The Hornets received Rice, point guard Khalid Reeves, center Matt Geiger, and a 1996 first-round draft choice. Mourning apparently changed his mind about the deal after a meeting with his college coach, John Thompson, the previous day.

When the trade was finalized, Mourning couldn't have been happier. He would be playing for Pat Riley, who had coached two superstar centers—Kareem Abdul-Jabbar in Los Angeles and Patrick Ewing in New York. Mourning was so anxious to play for Riley he said he would be ready for the Heat's season opener the following night against the Cleveland Cavaliers at the Miami Arena.

"I'm ready to get rolling," he said. "Once the jump ball goes up, I'll be able to put all this negative stuff behind me and make some things happen for myself and this organization. I came here with the intention of being here for the rest of my career."

As excited as Mourning was, the wily Riley reacted like someone who had just hit the lottery. "I think he has answered my prayers," he said, while trying to suppress a Cheshire cat grin over his uncanny ability to corner the market on top-flight centers. "This is a leap of faith. I believe this is a long-term relationship. This team needs a building block, a cornerstone. I had the opportunity to coach Kareem Abdul-Jabbar and Patrick Ewing, and I think the only place we can build a team is from within. He is considered a franchise player . . . well beyond an impact player."

Mourning was the type of player Riley needed and wanted to launch his first season in Miami. In 13 seasons with Los Angeles and New York, Riley had never won fewer than 50 games and had averaged 58 wins. In seven years of existence, the Heat had averaged only 29 wins and never had won more than 42 games. Riley had developed an aura of winning and a reputation as a defensive genius, and

Coach Pat Riley used Mourning's extensive talents as the cornerstone of a rebuilt Miami playoff team in 1996.

Mourning was a perfect fit. He had proven to be a winner at Charlotte, leading the Hornets to their first 50-victory season, and his defensive prowess as a shot-blocker and intimidator was renowned throughout the league.

Surprisingly, after joining the Heat, Mourning put his contract negotiations on hold. Taking the opposite stance he had assumed in Charlotte, he said he did not want to talk about money until after the season. He was counting on his strong play to enhance his bargaining position.

As soon as the trade for Mourning was announced, Miamians were struck with Heat fever. For a team that had created little excitement in Miami, standing third in popularity among the three major professional sports teams in the city—the others being the football Dolphins and the baseball Marlins—the Heat suddenly were a hot ticket.

The combination of Riley and Mourning helped attract a capacity crowd of 15,200 for the game against the Cleveland Cavaliers, not one of the NBA's marquee teams. "These nights just make you feel alive," Riley said.

Mourning also felt alive. Energized by the crowd and pumped up by Riley, he played 33 minutes, scored 15 points, and blocked five shots as the Heat beat the Cavaliers 85-71 at their own game—defense. Still, he was hardly satisfied. He had six turnovers, committed five fouls, and shot an air ball.

"I'm a little disappointed in the way I played," he said. "But it's going to come. The key to our success is going to be defense. We have enough young legs and young bodies that we should be able to move well so we can double-team and trap. We're going to be a team to be reckoned with. We're going to the playoffs."

They were going to the playoffs, but not with the team as it was constructed at that time. Riley, also the Heat's president, was not through reconfiguring the roster. On February 22, the trading deadline, the Heat was an embarrassing 24-29, and Riley was incensed. To try and turn around the Heat's fortunes, he swung three trades and signed veteran guard Jeff Malone. In the deals, he sent center Kevin Willis and point guard Bimbo Coles to the Golden State Warriors for point guard Tim Hardaway and forward-center Chris Gatling. He dealt forward Billy Owens and guard Kevin Gamble to the Sacramento Kings for forwards Walt Williams and Tyrone Corbin. And he traded guard Terrence Rencher to the Phoenix Suns for guard Tony Smith. Of the Heat's five starters, Riley had unloaded four—Owens, Williams, Coles, and Gamble. The only one who remained was Mourning.

After that, the rejuvenated Heat finished the season at 42-40 and beat out Mourning's old team, the Charlotte Hornets, by one game for the final playoff spot in the Eastern Conference. Flourishing under Riley, Mourning led the Heat in scoring (a career-high 23.2), rebounding (10.4), blocks (2.70), and minutes per game (38.2). He also made the All-Star team for the third straight year.

The playoffs were not nearly as pleasurable an experience as the regular season. In the opening round, Miami was matched against the eventual NBA champions, the Chicago Bulls, and were eliminated in three straight games. None of the games was close—102-85, 106-75, and 112-91. The Bulls virtually negated Mourning in the first two games.

After the season, Mourning and the Heat got around to discussing a new contract. On July 16, 1996, Mourning disclosed he had reached agreement on a seven-year, $112 million deal. As financially rewarding as that was to Mourning, it was costly for the Heat. Not only would it cost the team an average of $16 million per season for Mourning, it cost them the services of forward Juwan Howard, who had signed with Miami for $100.8 million. The league charged that the Heat had surpassed their salary cap with the combination of Mourning's and Howard's contracts, although Mourning contended he had not signed his deal. The NBA voided Howard's contract, and then he re-signed with the Washington Bullets, leaving the Heat with a huge void at forward.

Despite the loss of Howard and being swept in the playoffs by Chicago, Mourning faced the 1996-97 season and the future with optimism. He had supreme confidence in Riley's ability to produce a championship team. That's why he chose Miami over the other teams that were seeking his services when he left Charlotte.

"I looked at his track record," Mourning said. "Pretty much whatever he put his hands on turned to gold. He went to L.A. and they won; he was very successful out there. As soon as he set foot in New York, things changed. A team nobody ever thought could make it as far as they made it, he got them that close to winning a title. He made trades, he got the right personnel in there, and they did it. They got where a lot of guys dream of getting, and I want to have that opportunity."

Riley has duplicated that formula with the Heat. Helped by Mourning's 19-points-per-game

Alonzo Mourning celebrates after sinking a 2-pointer with only seconds left.

average, Miami made a big run for the title in the 1996-97 season. The Heat won a franchise-record 61 games, and reached the Eastern Conference finals before losing to eventual-NBA champions Chicago in five games. Riley was chosen coach of the year for the third time, reflecting his ability to get the Heat to play beyond their potential.

The 1997-98 season did not get off to a good start for Mourning. A partially-torn tendon in his left knee forced him to miss the first 22 games. Once he returned, however, he showed his old verve, scoring, rebounding, and blocking shots in his customary style.

Mourning can be assured that Riley will continue to do everything possible to make sure he has more opportunities to win a title in the future. Riley is a strong believer that everything should go through the center. Mourning is the Heat's center at least through the 2002-2003 season.

"He's the cornerstone," Riley said.

"I've been around a lot of great players, and there aren't many who care as much as he does. Sometimes his pride gets distorted. Some nights, as good as you may be, it's just not going your way. He's going to grow because he does whatever he has to to be better and make us better.

"But for him to get to the next level is for him to begin to finish all the other parts of his game to make his teammates better. A franchise player's value is how much better he makes other players because of his greatness. That's the key."

For a man who thrives on being the center of attention, those were encouraging words for Mourning. Now, all he has to do is live up to Riley's faith in him. As Mourning goes, so will go the Heat. He knows it and so do others. He has a whopping contract, huge responsibility, and an immense drive and desire to succeed.

"He has to do it," his friend and former college teammate, Dikembe Mutombo, said. "He's the man."

CHRONOLOGY

1970   Born February 8, in Chesapeake, Virginia.

1988   Announced he would attend Georgetown University in Washington, D.C.

1989   Led NCAA Division I in blocked shots with 169.

1992   Led NCAA Division I in blocked shots with 160; selected to the All-America team; selected by the Charlotte Hornets in the first round—second pick overall—in the NBA draft.

1993   Selected to the NBA All-Rookie team.

1994   Selected to the NBA Eastern Conference All-Star team.

1995   Selected to the NBA Eastern Conference All-Star team; traded by the Hornets with LeRon Ellis and Pete Myers to the Miami Heat for Glen Rice, Khalid Reeves, Matt Geiger, and a 1996 first-round draft choice.

1996   Selected to the NBA Eastern Conference All-Star team; was leading the Heat to their best season before an injury cut short his season.

1997   Selected to the NBA Eastern Conference All-Star team for the fourth consecutive time, but he did not play because of injury. He also missed the first 22 games of the 1997-98 season due to a torn tendon in his left knee.

STATISTICS

ALONZO MOURNING

College Statistics	G	Min	FGM	FGA	Pct	FTM	FTA	Pct	REB	AST	PTS	RPG	PPG
1988-89/Georgetown	34	962	158	262	.603	130	195	.667	248	24	447	7.3	13.1
89-90/Georgetown	31	937	145	276	.525	220	281	.783	265	36	510	8.5	16.5
90-91/Georgetown	23	682	105	201	.522	149	188	.793	178	25	363	7.7	15.8
91-92/Georgetown	32	1051	204	343	.595	272	359	.758	343	53	681	10.7	21.3
Totals	120	3632	612	1082	.561	771	1023	.750	1034	138	2001	8.6	16.7

Pro Statistics	G	Min	FGM	FGA	Pct	FTM	FTA	Pct	REB	AST	PTS	RPG	PPG
92-93/Charlotte	78	2644	572	1119	.511	485	634	.781	805	76	1639	10.3	21.0
93-94/Charlotte	60	2018	427	845	.505	433	568	.762	810	86	1287	10.2	21.5
94-95/Charlotte	77	2941	571	1101	.519	490	644	.761	761	111	1643	9.9	21.3
95-96/Miami	70	2671	563	1076	.523	488	712	.685	727	159	1623	10.4	23.2
96-97/Miami	66	2323	472	884	.534	364	567	.642	653	106	1307	9.9	19.8
Totals	351	12597	2605	5025	.518	2260	3125	.723	3756	538	7499	10.7	21.4

G	games
FGM	field goals made
FGA	field goals attempted
Pct	percent
FTM	free throws made
FTA	free throws attempted
REB	rebounds
AST	assists
PTS	points
RPG	rebounds per game
PPG	points per game

FURTHER READING

McCallum, Jack, "Middle Men," *Sports Illustrated*, April 17, 1993.

Taylor, Phil, "Learning Center," *Sports Illustrated*, Oct. 11, 1993.

ABOUT THE AUTHOR

Bert Rosenthal has been with The Associated Press since 1957. During that time, he has worked as a baseball statistician, a staffer in the Newark (N.J.) bureau, a sports writer on the Broadcast Desk and a writer in the Sports Department since 1970. Since 1973, he has been the AP's track and field writer, and from 1973-76, he also was the AP's pro basketball writer. He has covered every Summer Olympics since 1976 and every World Indoor and Outdoor Track and Field World Championship, plus several Pan American Games, World University Games and Commonwealth Games.

He also was the editor of *Hoop Magazine*, the official NBA publication, from 1976-80, has authored many books on sports personalities and individual sports, and has written for numerous magazines and other publications.

He lives in Scotch Plains, New Jersey, with his wife, Emily, and their two children, Sandra and Rebecca. He also has two other children, Gail and Scott.

INDEX

Photo Credits
AP/Wide World Photos: 2, 8, 11, 13, 16, 18, 21, 22, 24, 27, 28, 30, 32, 35, 36, 38, 40, 43, 47, 50,
53, 55, 59